T0011237

Why Do We Need TREES?

by Laura K. Murray

PEBBLE
a capstone imprint

Published by Pebble, an imprint of Capstone
1710 Roe Crest Drive, North Mankato, Minnesota 56003
capstonepub.com

Library of Congress Cataloging-in-Publication Data is available on the Library of Congress website.

ISBN: 9780756575519 (hardcover)
ISBN: 9780756575465 (paperback)
ISBN: 9780756575472 (ebook PDF)

Summary: Trees are great for shade in the summer. We also use them to build our homes. But what else do trees do? A lot! They help keep the air clean. They provide shelter for animals. And they can even help prevent landslides.

Editorial Credits
Editor: Ericka Smith; Designer: Kayla Rossow; Media Researcher: Svetlana Zhurkin; Production Specialist: Katy LaVigne

Image Credits
Dreamstime: Svitlana Imnadze, 4; Getty Images: Anna Rostova, 16, GMVozd, 27, imv, 10, Noel Hendrickson, 14; Shutterstock: Akintevs, 11 (right), AlohaHawaii, cover, Anne Coatesy, 18, Artishok (dotted background), cover and throughout, Clare Louise Jackson, 15, Dark_Side, 12, Enessa Varnaeva, 5, Faith Forrest (wood background), cover, back cover, and throughout, Herman Wong HM, 22 (middle), jurgal, 11 (left), K Steve Cope, 22 (bottom), Lesley Photograph, 13, Margrit Hirsch, 23, mark higgins, 29 (bottom), Mike Flippo, 20, Oleg Znamenskiy, 26, Paralaxis, 25, Peter J. Wilson, 24, Protasov AN, 17, Ragulina, 28, Simon Dannhauer, 29 (middle), Stanislav71, 6, tonyzhao120, 19, Triff, 9, varuna, 8, wavebreakmedia, 21, Will Pedro, 29 (top), Youra Pechkin, 7

Table of Contents

Words in **bold** are in the glossary.

Branching Out

It is early morning. Fog hangs over giant redwood trees. Sunlight shines through their branches. The trees can reach over 370 feet (113 meters). They are the tallest trees on Earth. Their roots stretch far and wide. They can live up to 2,000 years!

redwood trees

Trees make life possible. They make **oxygen** for us to breathe. They clean the water and air. They provide homes for wildlife. They help keep the planet healthy.

All About Trees

Trees are plants. They have a long, woody stem called a trunk. They come in all sizes. Redwoods are the tallest. Other trees are really short. The Arctic willow is only 6 to 8 inches (15 to 20 centimeters) tall.

Arctic willows

spruce trees

Some trees drop their leaves every year. Oak and maple trees are part of this group. Other trees are evergreen. They keep their leaves all year. Pine and spruce trees are evergreens.

A tree has three main parts. It has a crown, a trunk, and roots. The crown is also called the canopy. It is made up of branches and leaves. Branches grow from the trunk.

crown

trunk

roots

Leaves make food for the tree. They take in water and **carbon dioxide**. They use sunlight to make it into food. This process also makes oxygen.

Roots keep a tree in place. They take in water, **nutrients**, and **minerals** from the soil.

Trees begin as seeds. Seeds can be inside an acorn or nut. Some trees have seeds inside their fruit, like cherries. Other trees have seeds inside their cones.

A sprout grows from an acorn.

seedling

sapling

Soil, water, air, and sun help the seed grow into a sprout. It stretches roots into the soil. The sprout becomes a seedling. It grows bark. The seedling grows into a young tree called a sapling. Then it becomes an adult tree. Eventually, it spreads its own seeds.

The green color of leaves comes from **chlorophyll**. It helps plants make their food. Leaves also have yellow and orange colors. But often the green color covers them up.

Many leaves have bright colors in the fall. Temperatures drop. Leaves stop making food. The green color breaks down. Yellow and orange colors are easier to see. Some leaves become red, pink, or purple.

How Do Trees Help Us?

Most living things need oxygen to survive. This includes humans. Most oxygen comes from the ocean. But some comes from trees. Trees give off oxygen as they make food. A large tree can create enough oxygen for four people for one day.

Trees also help clean the air. Too much carbon dioxide is harmful to the planet. Carbon dioxide in the air comes from things like cars and power plants. Trees take it out of the air. They store it inside.

Trees are important to Earth's water systems. They take in water when it rains a lot. This helps stop flooding. Then they slowly let the water back into the ground and the air.

Trees also clean and filter water. They catch dust before it gets into lakes and streams. And their roots take out harmful pollutants.

Roots have other important jobs.
They hold the soil together. This can
help keep **landslides** from happening.

Trees are home to many kinds of wildlife. Bats, birds, snakes, koalas, and bugs are just some of the animals that live in trees.

Dead trees are important too! They are called snags. They become a log when they fall. They help new plants grow.

Trees also make food for humans and animals. They grow apples, bananas, walnuts, and much more. Animals eat the bark, leaves, and other parts.

People use trees for all kinds of products. They use trees for things like lumber and fuel. They make paper from trees too.

Some people use trees for medicine. They might use the wood, bark, or fruit of a tree. Humans have used willow bark as medicine for thousands of years. It treats pain and fever.

Trees are useful in other ways too.
They provide shade. They block the
wind. They can even boost your mood!
They can help you feel calm.

Threats to Trees

Today many trees are in danger. Pests are a big threat. The emerald ash borer is a beetle that feeds on ash trees. It has killed millions of trees.

an emerald ash borer

damage from emerald ash borers

Disease is another threat. Trees can survive many illnesses. But new diseases are taking over. They attack a tree's leaves, roots, and other parts. They spread quickly.

People can help stop the spread of pests and disease. One way to help is by not moving firewood from place to place.

Weather can be a threat to trees. **Droughts**, floods, and storms can destroy trees. Forest fires are a big problem. They destroy millions of acres each year. And **climate change** is making things worse.

People harm trees too. Sometimes people do not take care of forests. They cut down too many trees. And they use chemicals and **pesticides** that can harm trees.

A World Without Trees

Can you imagine a world without trees? Living things would slowly die. People and wildlife would not have the clean air they need. Floods could wash away the land.

Many animals would lose their homes and food. Foods like maple syrup and cocoa would not exist. Books, gum, and other products made from trees would be different.

Trees have many important jobs, like cleaning the air and providing homes to birds. Humans and wildlife depend on trees. They're nature we need!

baobab trees

COOL FACTS ABOUT TREES

- The study of trees and other woody plants is called *dendrology*.

- Great Basin bristlecone pine trees can live for thousands of years. Scientists believe that one cut down in Nevada was 4,700 to 5,000 years old.

- Tree rings can show how old a tree was, what the weather was like during its life, and other information.

- The General Sherman sequoia tree is the world's largest tree by volume. It is 275 feet (83.8 m) tall and more than 36 feet (11 m) wide.

- One apple tree may take in as many as 95 gallons (360 liters) of water from the soil every day.

- Koalas eat the leaves of eucalyptus trees.

Glossary

carbon dioxide (KAHR-buhn dy-AHK-syd)—a gas in the air that animals give off and plants use to make food

chlorophyll (KLOR-uh-fil)—the green substance in plants that uses light to make food from carbon dioxide and water

climate change (KLY-muht CHAYNJ)—a significant change in Earth's climate over a period of time

drought (DROUT)—a long period of weather with little or no rainfall

landslide (LAND-slide)—a large mass of earth and rocks that suddenly slides down a mountain or hill

mineral (MIN-ur-uhl)—a material found in nature that is not an animal or a plant

nutrient (NOO-tree-uhnt)—something that is needed by people, animals, and plants to stay healthy and strong

oxygen (OK-suh-juhn)—a colorless gas that people and animals breathe; people and animals need oxygen to live

pesticide (PES-tuh-side)—a poisonous chemical used to kill insects, rats, and fungi that can damage plants

Read More

Bergin, Raymond. *Forest Life Connections.*
Minneapolis: Bearport Publishing, 2023.

Fox, Kate Allen. *Pando: A Living Wonder of Trees.*
North Mankato, MN: Capstone, 2021.

Hudd, Emily. *How Long Does a Redwood Tree Live?*
North Mankato, MN: Capstone, 2020.

Internet Sites

DK Find Out!: Trees
dkfindout.com/us/animals-and-nature/plants/trees

Kids Do Ecology: Temperate Forest
kids.nceas.ucsb.edu/biomes/temperateforest.html

NASA Climate Kids: What Can Trees Tell Us About Climate Change?
climatekids.nasa.gov/tree-rings

Index

About the Author

Laura K. Murray is the Minnesota-based author of more than 100 published or forthcoming books for young readers. She loves learning from fellow readers and helping others find their reading superpowers! Visit her at LauraKMurray.com.